Spiritual Dangers

DAG HEWARD-MILLS

Parchment House

First published 2013 by Parchment House
3rd Printing 2014

Find out more about Dag Heward-Mills at:

Healing Jesus Campaign
Write to: evangelist@daghewardmills.org
Website: www.daghewardmills.org
Facebook: Dag Heward-Mills
Twitter: @EvangelistDag

ISBN: 978-9988-8550-4-8

Contents

Contents

Chapter 1

Why Certain Things Must Be Done First

Wrong priorities are great dangers for Christians. When you are a sinner, you basically choose between two opinions: good and evil. As you grow in the Lord, your options increase and you begin to have more to choose from.

This time your choices are not between good and evil but between good and good. In terms of what to do, there are often several good things to choose from. When you get to that point it is important that you understand the concept of priorities: "Which one do I do first?" Jesus gave us a great revelation on some things that should be done before others.

It is interesting to study how many things Jesus said should be done first. Whenever Jesus spoke of the first or the foremost issue, He used the Greek word *proton*. In this book, we take a look at the *proton* issues; *things that Jesus said should be done first.*

As a Christian, you must do first things first. First things first means first in time, order, number, rank and value.

A Christian must do *the* most important things first.

Why Must Certain Things Be Done First?

1. Anything that is not done first seems to lose its significance.

God is very patient with us. Many have disobeyed Him and seem to have gotten away with it. The importance of the Word of God seems to fade as we carry on in disobedience. Very soon that which is more important than anything else becomes despised and irrelevant.

Today, I minister under the anointing and many respect me for the ministry. But if I had not obeyed God when I did, I may have lived out my life normally as a medical doctor. Discussions about the call of God would have seemed insignificant and irrelevant.

Sitting amongst my medical colleagues in various hospitals, the thought of being a pastor would have sounded ridiculous. I would have said to my friends, "Let me tell you about a silly idea I once had. Did you know that I once wanted to be a pastor? When we were younger, we were over- spiritual and impractical."

Have you never met grown-ups who said they were originally lined up for priesthood? In their old age they try to compensate for their disobedience through their children.

I know a man who tried to force one of his children to become a priest.

He said to his son, "God called me to be a priest but I didn't do it. You become that priest and I will give you property and money so that you lack nothing." At the end of their lives they desperately want to compensate for a life of non-compliance and non-cooperation with God.

Dear friend, I can assure you that the longer you walk in your own ways the more distant and unrealistic the commands of God will seem. There is a reason for *proton.*

Proton, doing first things first, saves you from deception. God will take care of you and be with you as you flow in His will.

2.   Anything that is not done first may never be done.

Delay often means cancellation. Anything that is not done first may never be done. I never knew that delaying something could actually lead to its cancellation.

There was a day I had to make a trip from London to New York to minister. I was actually scheduled to minister in Maryland that night. Unfortunately, I had a very early flight from Heathrow Airport in London, to Amsterdam and then I was to connect from Amsterdam to New York. Somehow I did not believe the time I saw on my ticket. I thought it was too early to be true.

When I got to the airport, for the first time in my life, I was too late to check-in or to board the aircraft. I had missed the check-in time by about twenty minutes. I was disappointed. I had to wait for the next flight to Amsterdam!

"You cannot make your first connection to New York but you can get a later flight," they told me. I realized from the time, that I would still make it to New York and just in time to drive to Maryland. So I called New York and told the pastor when I would be arriving and told him that we would need to drive rapidly to Maryland. I assured him that we were in good time and that the programme would surely come on in spite of the slight delay.

In Amsterdam, I confidently boarded my connecting flight to New York knowing that it would soon take off and I would be on my way. After a while, I looked out of the window and I saw people spraying the wings of the plane. Then came the announcement: "There is so much ice on the engine that it will not be safe to take off. It will take us one hour to get rid of it. Please bear with us."

I did another calculation and I still felt I could just make it to Maryland for the programme. The whole church would be waiting for me. They had been expecting me for weeks. Unfortunately, it was not to be so.

After the ice problem was solved, a new one arose, introducing even further delays. This time they said the toilets in the plane were not working and they had to fix them. I had never heard of toilets in a plane not working but it was happening live! It took another two hours before we were finally ready for take-off.

I sat in anguish as the minutes went by, imagining how many people would have gathered for the programme. Eventually, I had to accept that the programme would be cancelled because I would not make it in time. As I sat in my chair, I reflected over how the twenty-minute delay in London had cancelled my entire programme.

It was then that the Lord spoke to me: *"Do you see that delay can mean cancellation?"*

The Lord showed me that the delay in obeying His Word could lead to my never doing His will! The Lord showed me that He had allowed me to have this experience so that I would learn how the delay in doing His will sometimes leads to my never doing it.

Many who intend to obey God will never end up obeying Him because they put the wrong things first. Their marriage, their PhDs, their MBAs, and their five-year trip abroad, all come before obedience to the Lord. Obedience to God, which they put in second place never materialized.

I have watched with sadness as people who should have been full-time in the ministry postpone it till after they accomplished certain things. Unfortunately that delay permanently closed the opportunity for them to be in full-time ministry. What people don't realize is that with time, circumstances change so much that the will of God does not seem realistic any more.

Delay often means cancellation but many do not know this fact. Has God spoken to you? What has He asked you to do? Maybe obeying God is not proton for you. Perhaps a thousand different things come before your obedience to the Lord.

3. It is an insult to give the second place to that which should be first.

Many do not realize that it is insulting to make God your second or third option.

One day while I was preaching, I identified several young ladies who did not have husbands.

I suggested to them to get married to a nice young man in church. They all refused.

"Why don't you want to marry him, is he not a handsome man?"

"Yes he is," they answered.

4

"Is he a spiritual person?"

"Yes he is. He is even a pastor."

"Does he not have a car and a house?"

"Yes he does. Actually his car is very nice."

"Then why don't any of you want to marry him?"

"Because he has a wife already," they answered.

I continued, "But you can be his second wife?"

In chorus they all cried out, *"No way, no sir, we will not be second wives, we want to be number one."*

They felt insulted that I would offer them the second position. They wanted to be wives but not second wives. These young ladies wanted to be wives but only if they would be the first and only wives. This is how God feels. He knows we will serve Him but He wants us to serve Him first. It is actually an insult to put God after anything! Unfortunately, God is constantly relegated to the second, third and sometimes tenth place of importance. It is time for God to take His proton (foremost) position in your life.

4. Problems abound when that which is to be first becomes second.

When something that is supposed to be done second is done first, many things go wrong. I was recently in one African country and my host took me to a cemetery. I was amazed at the fresh graves that were gradually filling every space. At a dinner, with another pastor friend, he gave me an incredible account of the number of funerals that he was conducting in his city. He told us that they had so many funerals that pastors no longer conducted funeral services. The funerals were so numerous that cell leaders had to conduct burial services of church members.

I listened in amazement. He went on to describe how they no longer buried people lying down because there was no space in the cemetery. He described how they buried them vertically, standing up! The coffins were actually placed vertically into the ground to save space. In other words, the dead bodies would stand, rather than lie down. I thought to myself, "In such a situation do you say, 'stand in peace,' or 'rest in peace'?"

What was the cause of this unprecedented wave of death in this country? Why were so many people dying?

The answer was simple: the second thing had come before the first thing. Sex had come before marriage. Sex is supposed to be experienced only after marriage. In this country, sex was an experience occurring largely outside the context of marriage. A wave of death had swept through that nation because the first thing had become the second and the second thing first.

Chapter 2

Why the Kingdom of God Must Be Your First Passion

But seek ye first (PROTON) the kingdom of God, and his righteousness; and all these things shall be added unto you.

Matthew 6:33

God wants the first part of everyone's life. The first part of our lives is the season of productivity. It is the period in which people abound in faith, hope, love and fertility.

Seek the kingdom of God before you seek your personal kingdom of wealth, comfort and security. There are many reasons why the kingdom of God must be sought first and in the first part of your life.

1. The kingdom of God requires an early start. The kingdom of Heaven also requires a lot of time and attention.

The commonest characteristic of large churches is that the pastor has been there for many years. It takes a long time to grow a congregation from the fellowship stage to the mega church stage. If you think that the work of God can be done in a few weeks, or months, you deceive yourself and the truth is not in you. It takes many years for something substantial to be accomplished in ministry.

Let me give you an exercise. Take any well known and large ministry and find out when the pastor really began his ministry. Jesus Himself began His preparation for ministry as a child. Samuel the prophet was brought to the temple as a child. The preparation takes many years.

This is why Levites became priests only by the age of thirty.

From THIRTY YEARS OLD and upward even until fifty years old, all that enter into the host, to do the work in the tabernacle of the congregation.

Numbers 4:3

This is why Jesus started His ministry by the age of thirty:

And Jesus himself began to be about THIRTY YEARS OF AGE, being (as was supposed) the son of Joseph, which was the son of Heli,

Luke 3:23

Because the work of God requires so much time both for preparation and actual ministry, it must be the first thing in your life.

Many people put off the ministry because they actually despise it; they feel that it is something that can be done within a short time.

2. The kingdom needs young people.

There are many things that only young people can do. There are things I did when I was younger that I cannot do today. For instance, I remember when I was in secondary school, I fasted for almost one school term. I wonder if I could do something like that today.

I used to hold "dawn-broadcasts" (open-air preaching at dawn) in many places. As a student, I did many exciting things for the Lord. All night prayer meetings, dawn broadcasts, twelve-hour prayer meetings, seven-hour prayer meetings etc. Although I basically do the same things today, there are obvious changes in the intensity and style.

I really cherish the more youthful years I spent in Christ. In those years I memorized entire chapters of the Bible. It is the verses I learnt in those days that form the basis of my Scripture knowledge today.

Perhaps you do not know why God wants you to take Him as the first thing in the first part of your life. Perhaps you want to give God your years of weakness and trembling. The first part is the best part: when you are strong, energetic and zealous. That is the part that God wants!

3. The kingdom of God needs faith, hope, and love.

Remember now thy Creator in the days of thy youth, while the evil days come not, nor the years draw nigh, when thou shalt say, I have no pleasure in them;

Ecclesiastes 12:1

The kingdom of God needs energetic people for the ministry. There is a lot of stress and strain in the ministry. Contrary to what people think, pastors are often very stressed and very tired. They rarely have time for themselves and their families.

In the first part of your life you are full of faith, hope and love. Watch the older people and you will notice that they have less "spring in their gait". Tiredness and weariness has set in. Bad experiences have made them weary and suspicious of everyone. They trust no one and are unwilling to try new things. The spirit of adventure is gone. They are hardened by their lives' experiences. Older people have seen pain, bitterness and death. Yes, they believe in God but it is a little different from a younger person's faith.

In the first part of your life, you are not yet broken-hearted. It is this part that God badly wants. God wants the first part of your life. The book of Ecclesiastes, Chapter 12, aptly describes this.

Keep your creator in mind while you are young! In years to come, you will be burdened down with troubles and say, "I don't enjoy life anymore."

Your body will grow feeble, your teeth will decay, and your eyesight fail.

The noisy grinding of grain will be shut out by your deaf ears, but even the song of a bird will keep you awake. You will be afraid to climb up a hill or walk down a road.

Your hair will turn as white as almond blossoms. You will feel lifeless and drag along like an old grasshopper...

Ecclesiastes 12:1,3-5
(Contemporary English version)

It is said that King Solomon wrote the book of Song of Solomon in his youth, the book of Proverbs in his middle age and the book of Ecclesiastes in his older years. You will notice that the mood of each of these books is different. In the Song of Solomon, he is excited and in love. In the book of Proverbs, he shares practical wisdom for regular life. But in the book of Ecclesiastes, his mood is quite different. He describes many of life's experiences as inconsequential, vain and futile.

Nothing makes sense, I have seen it all—nothing makes sense.

Ecclestiastes 12:8
(Contemporary English version)

This drop in mood greatly affects the work of God. It takes faith and hope in Heaven to take up your cross and sacrifice for an unseen God.

I enjoy the company of the younger Christian leaders in my church. They seem to enjoy what I preach more than the older ones. Many times they crowd around me after church just wanting to chat with me. They seem to believe everything I say, no matter how hard it sounds.

I remember one day in particular, I was talking to a group of older pastors. The younger university folks gathered around me as usual. As I continued chatting with them, I noticed as the older ones slunk away one after the other until I was left with only the young people. I wasn't saying anything in particular that pertained to young people, but the older guys were just not interested.

In the first part of your life you are very responsive, zealous and teachable. God can reach out to you and turn you in almost any direction. As you get older you become uninterested and disillusioned. There seems to be a teachable and humble spirit in the first part of our lives.

4. The kingdom of God cannot be despised.

There are many jobs that require job-seekers to be below the age of thirty. Why do you think many companies recruit people below a certain age? Because they want to get the best out of them!

Don't despise the church. There are people who say they will work for God when they retire. Which occupation can be compared with the high calling of ministry? Medicine, law, engineering, architecture, carpentry, computing, banking, journalism, research, pharmacy, mining, management, acting, singing, dancing, plumbing, masonry or piloting cannot be compared with the ministry of the Lord Jesus Christ.

But what things were gain to me, those I counted loss for Christ Yea doubtless, and I count all things but loss for the excellency of the knowledge of Christ Jesus my Lord: for whom I have suffered the loss of all things, and do count them but dung, that I may win Christ,

Philippians 3:7-8

The priesthood is the high calling of God. And that is what I am involved with. On this earth, the priesthood is despised. I once had a pastor who couldn't find a wife because he was a pastor. The mother of his would-be bride, refused to allow her daughter to be engaged to a pastor. She felt that a pastor was an aimless, jobless man without prospects.

On one occasion, she even sent an emissary to find out if he really worked with the church as he claimed. She also wanted to find out what kind of work he could possibly be doing. The bride's mother's envoy could not hide her surprise when she found out that the church actually had offices and that there was a lot of work going on in these offices.

5. The kingdom cannot be delayed.

Some people think their marriages cannot be delayed, their schools cannot be delayed and their work cannot be delayed. But let me tell you what cannot be delayed: the kingdom of God! Jesus said we should not say that there are yet four months till the harvest. In other words don't say that there is more time. Don't introduce delays for the kingdom of God.

Say not ye, There are yet four months, and then cometh harvest? Behold, I say unto you, Lift up your eyes, and look on the fields; for they are white already to harvest.

John 4:35

Unknown to many people, this earthly life is very time-related. Every instruction or opportunity is time-related. Hear this and hear it very well: every instruction that God has given to you has an invisible timer on it. A countdown begins from the moment God speaks to you. The available time to perform that duty reduces with every passing hour. Many think they are just biding their time and will take God seriously later. Do not be deceived! The expiry date of your grace period is fast approaching.

When Princess Diana was going out with her Egyptian boyfriend, she didn't know that she had a few more hours to live. She was oblivious to the fact that she was to be the subject of the largest funeral of all time. She didn't know the time. Do you know the time? Do we know the time?

If God has called you to the ministry a clock has begun to tick. A time will come when you will no longer be able to fulfil that instruction. Sometimes God speaks to you, "Finance my Kingdom." Perhaps that comes along with a five-year period wherein you can obey Him.

Perhaps He tells you, "Go out as a missionary." Maybe that has a ten-year period wherein you could fulfil it. Some people spend seven years of that period doing other things and then in the last three years attempt to obey God. But their time is almost up. Nothing effective can be done in the remaining three years.

6. Jesus rejects all those who put their family, business or personal wealth before the kingdom of God.

And sent his servant at supper time to say to them that were bidden, Come; for all things are now ready. And they all with one consent began to make excuse. The first said unto him, I HAVE BOUGHT A PIECE OF GROUND, and I must needs go and see it: I pray thee have me excused. And another said, I HAVE BOUGHT FIVE YOKE OF OXEN, and I go to prove them: I pray thee have me excused. And another said, I HAVE MARRIED A WIFE, and therefore I cannot come.

Luke 14:17-20

Many decent Christians hide behind their families or legitimate businesses to stay away from obeying God.

Unfortunately, Jesus specifically mentions these things as reasons that will not stand before Him. Nothing and I mean nothing is more important than God and our service to Him. When God calls you, you have no right to use your wife, husband or children as a reason to stay away. When God calls for you, you have no right to use your business or personal wealth as a reason to stay away.

Read it for yourself. Contrary to what many dignified and self-righteous people think, your service to God is more important than any of these things.

John Wesley, the founder of the Methodist church had major problems with his wife. She did not want him to continue corresponding with some of the congregants in his parish. John Wesley preached on Sunday, got married on Monday and preached the next day. In less than a month, he was on the road again. Neither wife nor family could stop him from doing what his heart loved most. Today, the Methodist Church stands as a veritable testimony to the unyielding commitment of John Wesley to the things of God.

Chapter 3

The Danger of Fornication

But fornication, and all uncleanness, or covetousness, let it not be once named among you, as becometh saints;

Ephesians 5:3

Fornication is sexual intercourse before marriage. The equivalent of fornication in marriage is adultery, that is, when you have sex with anyone who is not your marriage partner.

Although most of us pastors are silent on this subject, it is important that we also speak about it. In Jeremiah 3:15, the Lord said, "And, I will give you pastors according to mine heart, which shall feed you with knowledge and understanding." Being a pastor of God's flock means teaching on a wide range of subjects.

I must admit that, when the Lord first led me to write a book on this subject, I was a bit hesitant. This is because I am a human being and I am subject to the same temptations as everyone else. But it is important to obey God's Word and teach all the things that are in the Bible.

God's standard for the Christian life is that no believer should ever be involved in fornication. Christians should not have a history of regularly committing fornication.

Neither should they ever be involved in it. Not even once!

... fornication ... not be once named ...

Ephesians 5:3

Fornication is commonly found amongst born-again Christians. This "cancer" of fornication is rapidly affecting the body of Christ, because many Christians who get involved in fornication do not know its spiritual and physical implications.

Fornication is the ministry of a strange woman. She is out to bring you to that place. She is out to take advantage of the man's physiological needs. She is there to corrupt the church with her

14

fornication. The strange woman is there to drink the blood of prophets and apostles by sleeping with them.

How Fornication Corrupts and Destroys the Church

1. Fornication is disobedience.

The first reason why you should not commit fornication is that it is disobedience to God.

... Behold, to obey is better than sacrifice, and to hearken than the fat of rams.

1 Samuel 15:22

We are all subject to the temptation to fornicate. But the priority of every Christian must be to obey the Lord. If you do not obey God you stand to lose.

Obedience means more to God than any great sacrifice that you can make to Him. Some of you come to church, put your offering in the basket, pay your tithes, lift up your hands and worship His Majesty. You give sacrifices of praise to God. But God prefers your simple obedience to your many offerings and lifted hands.

I once met a lady who told me that the commandment not to commit fornication is an old fashioned law, meant for the olden days. She argued that it was no longer a realistic instruction. Even if it does not make sense to you, your duty is still to obey God.

Christianity has to do with your relationship with the Lord. As a Christian you are dependent on God, and it is only the Lord who can bless you. If you choose to disobey and disregard God, I do not know what kind of relationship you want to have with Him. When you disobey God, you incur God's curses upon your life.

Some people complain that it is difficult to obey God. "It costs so much," they say. Dear friend, the truth is that it pays to obey God but it costs to disobey Him.

As you read the rest of this book, you will realize that when God gives us a commandment, it is for our own good. It pays to obey God but it is very expensive to disobey Him.

2. Fornication will destroy your soul.

But whoso committeth adultery with a woman lacketh understanding: he that doeth it DESTROYETH his own SOUL.

Proverbs 6:32

When you commit fornication, the Bible says you will destroy your soul.

This means that fornication will have an effect on you spiritually. Anybody who is involved in fornication gets affected spiritually. You may not know exactly how it affects you. But it does affect you, and will lead you to backslide. On Sunday mornings there are people sitting in church knowing very well what they did the night before.

Some Christians even come to church straight from their boyfriends' beds. Your pastor may not know what you have done. He may have shaken hands with you, but did not have any word of knowledge about you! So you continue in sin. Know that it is gradually destroying your soul—**your inner self is affected!**

With experience, I have come to see that when somebody commits fornication, his spiritual life takes a nosedive. When a Christian falls into immorality his lifestyle changes. **The destruction of the soul has begun.**

3. Fornication will destroy your body.

Flee fornication. Every sin that a man doeth is without the body; but he that committeth fornication sinneth *against* his own *body*.

1 Corinthians 6:18

When you commit fornication you commit sin directly against your own body. When you commit fornication you commit a crime against your body. You are destroying your body.

If you commit a crime against the State, you are said to be destroying the State. That is why the State will arrest and prosecute you. In the same way when you commit fornication, you commit a *crime* against your body, and God *will* prosecute you for that.

> **... know ye not that your body is the temple of the Holy Ghost...?**
>
> **1 Corinthians 6:19**

4. You make covenants with all sorts of people.

Sex is intended to be a binding experience between two people. Know that when you commit fornication, you make a covenant with whoever you had sex with. God's plan is that when a woman has sex for the first time, her hymen is broken and blood is shed. Whenever blood is shed some sort of agreement or covenant is created.

That means when you have sex with different people, you may actually be entering into union with them. Agreements are made because blood is shed. That is one of the reasons why Paul asked:

> **... shall I then take the members of Christ, and make them the members of an harlot? God forbid.**
>
> **1 Corinthians 6:15**

Such covenants are for real. They can affect you for the rest of your life. I have seen people who have been crippled all their Christian lives because of fornication. **Some Christians never rise out of the covenant of fornication.**

The son of a fetish priest came to our church some years ago. He told us how he got involved in witchcraft. He said he once slept in the cemetery with his father.

After seven days his father cut his hand, drew his blood and mixed it with his own. Then they both drank the blood and made a permanent agreement. A covenant of witchcraft! This brother was under that covenant. A time came when he had to decide between his father, (that is following the fetish) and following Christ. This young man could not break away from this blood covenant. Friend, I am talking here about blood covenants! He left the church after some months and went back to his father's shrine.

Although he was born again, and knew the Lord, he could not easily break away from his covenant.

Blood and covenants are real things so do not sleep with just anybody. You may be sleeping with a witch and that witch will be in your home all the days of your life.

5. **Fornication brings evil spirits into your life.**

   ... Babylon the great... is become the habitation of devils, and the hold of every foul spirit, and a cage of every unclean and hateful bird.

   Revelation 18:2

A stronghold of evil spirits is a *refuge,* a *sanctuary* or a *hiding place* for demons. Why did so many evil spirits come to live in Babylon? Why has Babylon become a hold of demons?

According to Revelation 18:3:

For all nations have drunk of the wine of the wrath of her fornication, and the kings of the earth have committed fornication with her ...

The kings, the ministers of state, the rich and the famous have committed fornication with her. That is why evil spirits have come into her life. Fornication attracts evil spirits into your life. This is so true of many Christians' lives. Evil spirits have aggregated and congregated in them because of their fornication.

When God says do not do something He knows why! Some of the evil spirits that come into you can prevent you from ever getting married. Some evil spirits can cause you to backslide. Some of them will cause you to marry the wrong person. Some of them can cause you to have a bad marriage. Some of these evil spirits can also lead you into unfaithfulness in your marriage. The list is endless.

Do you want to become a hiding place for demons?

6. Fornication brings sickness.

There are a host of diseases that only come about through sexual intercourse. We call these STDs (sexually transmitted diseases). The germs that cause these diseases will have access into you when you commit fornication.

Let me mention only ten of them. (Please notice how big the names of these "animals" are!):

1. **Neisseria gonococcus** — this causes Gonorrhoea.

2. **Treponema pallidum** — this causes Syphilis.

3. **Chlamydia trachomatis** — this causes Non-Specific Urethritis.

4. **Hepatitis "B" virus** — this causes Liver diseases.

5. **Herpes simplex type II virus** — this causes Herpes Genitalis.

6. **Trichomonas vaginalis** — this causes Vaginitis.

7. **Lymphogranuloma venereum**

8. **Haemophilus ducreyii** — this causes Soft Sore (Chancroid).

9. **Urinary tract infection**

10. **Cancer of the cervix** — frequent sex at an early age predisposes you to cancer of the cervix.

If you wait till you marry before having sex, you may save yourself from all these diseases. But if you continue to commit fornication, then remember that all these "animals" will enter your body and make you sick!

7. Fornication brings death.

Fornication will kill you if you acquire the Human Immuno Virus (HIV). Unless God works a miracle, you may die of AIDS.

HIV is now a death sentence. It is sad to say that in the charismatic churches there are many Christians who are HIV positive.

A laboratory technician once gave me some alarming statistics. A team of lab technicians organized a blood donation event in a charismatic church and out of about a hundred people who donated blood, a large percentage tested positive for HIV. In other words, our churches have significant numbers of people with the HIV virus. Fornicating with your fellow church member may mean your death! Those who are HIV positive can develop AIDS. And when you have AIDS, it means you have a few more years to live.

8. Fornication brings unwanted pregnancies.

Do you want to attend school with your child? When I was in secondary school, there was a man in the sixth form who was said to have a child in form one. How could this be? Probably due to an unwanted pregnancy earlier on in his life.

9. Fornication brings unwanted abortions.

If you commit fornication and become pregnant, it is most likely that you will want to hide it—by committing abortion.

You are falling into the same trap that David fell into when he committed adultery. Murder is the commonest evil that follows the sin of fornication.

Abortion is the sin of murder. Many fornicators are murderers. Multiple abortionists are multiple murderers. Dear friend, you may not know that abortion is murder. Medically speaking, abortion is the termination of human life. The human life may be just a few cells, but it is human life! Are you a murderer?

10. Fornication brings infertility.

Let me explain how fornication brings infertility.

During an abortion, various instruments similar to knives and forks are introduced into the womb. This often leads to infection. And this infection often leads to blocking of the fallopian tubes. Young lady, if your fallopian tubes are blocked you will not be able to become pregnant.

Then you may find yourself in every deliverance centre— looking for healing. Receive your deliverance now by obeying the Word.

11. Fornication brings unwanted children.

Unwanted children are usually products of fornication. Why should you be pregnant when you are a sixteen-year-old student? Your child is supposed to be your daughter or son and not your younger sister or brother!

12. The unwanted children become social deviants.

Whenever a child is not wanted, he becomes a reject in society – a "*pikin na bollo*" as we say in Ghana. Many deviants in society have a background of having been unwanted.

I remember a young boy who beat up his mother and left home. No one knows where he is. I asked why a young sixth-former should behave in this unbecoming manner. The answer can be traced to his mother's history.

This young lad was a product of his mother's fornication when she was only fifteen years old. The boy had been made to stay with different aunties and other relatives. You see, his mother had to continue schooling. When his mother eventually got married, she was ashamed of her unwanted child. So he continued staying with other sympathetic relatives.

Naturally, the young lad grew up doing very poorly in school. He was suspended several times and became what we call a social deviant, a very bitter boy. Now whose fault is it? Do not blame any child who is born out of fornication if he becomes a social deviant!

13. Fornication brings disgrace.

A wound and dishonour shall he get; and his reproach shall not be wiped away.

Proverbs 6:33

Although fornication is an *international* and *cross-cultural* sin committed by many people—it is still a disgraceful act. Save yourself from this disgrace!

14. Fornication brings hurts and wounds.

Read the story of Tamar and Amnon in the second book of Samuel, chapter 13. Fornication leads to many *hurts*. Tamar was *hurt*. Absalom her brother was *hurt*. King David was hurt. The relationship between Tamar and Amnon was broken forever.

What you must realize is that fornication is essentially wrong and evil. It only leads to many terrible and devastating complications in life.

15. Fornication breaks marriages.

Fornication is often the last straw that breaks the camel's back in unhappy marriages. Remember, it is only in the case of adultery that God allows divorce.

God knows that this is the sin which has the ability to destroy marriages.

Chapter 4

Steps to Avoiding Fornication

How can we save ourselves from this disgraceful sin? We are all men of like passions subject to the same temptations as everyone else.

I believe the Lord has shown me some important steps that will keep us all from sin. Four of these steps are spiritual and six are physical. Let us start with the physical steps.

1. No untimely relationships

Very young people should not enter into relationships for courtship.

To every thing there is a season, and a time to every purpose under the heaven:

Ecclesiastes 3:1

There is a time for entering into a relationship. Why do you want to enter into a relationship when you are still in school? You do not even have a job in sight!

In my church, I do not recognize relationships of teenagers. I will advise you to break it in the name of Jesus! You worry yourself for nothing when you play with relationships at the wrong time.

2. Relationships only unto marriage

You must only enter into relationships that lead to marriage. *The only intimate relationship between men and women that God approves of is marriage.*

A Christian man and woman must move towards God's plan, and God's plan is marriage. When I proposed to my wife many years before I actually married her, I asked her two questions: "Can you marry a doctor? Can you marry a pastor?" Marriage was what I had in mind. She was in love with me so she said yes! I had decided that I was going to marry her. She was not just a friend or girlfriend. She had passed on to become someone special—the person who was going to be my wife and the bearer of my children.

I remember asking a young man who had been in a relationship with a sister in church for two years, "Are you getting married?" His response was "I don't think we will. We are just in a relationship."

I think a lady must be foolish to be in such a relationship. The man is just using you, and will throw you away one day. The relationships that God approves of are relationships that are headed towards His will; and His will is marriage!

If you know that your relationship is not going towards marriage, then it is just going towards fornication. Stop right there!

3. Holy relationships

The Bible says there is a time to "refrain from embracing."

... a time to embrace, and a time to refrain from embracing;

Ecclesiastes 3:5

If you are in a relationship, there is a time to refrain from embracing. I can hold my wife, I can hug her and I will not be doing anything wrong. But those of you who are not married are not expected to do so. Even when you touch your fiancée's hand, "osmosis" begins to occur!

In my church we have a few rules for counselling young people in relationships. We do not just tell you to live a holy and a pure life, but you are specifically told what living holy entails. You must only have holy relationships!

4. Early marriage

I encourage people to marry young. The more Christians delay the marriage ceremony, the more likely they are to end up

24

living in sin. What are you waiting for? In certain churches there are road blocks to marriage. Couples are presented with so many obstacles to delay marriage. But that should not be the case.

Let thy fountain be blessed: and rejoice with the wife of thy YOUTH.

Proverbs 5:18

The Scripture encourages you to have a wife when you are young—the wife of your youth.

Do not use the lack of money as an excuse, because you can marry if you really want to. Marry whilst you are still young. Do not wait until you have all the comfortable things in life before venturing into marriage.

When I decided to get married, somebody whispered to my wife to marry someone who had everything in life. I certainly did not qualify because I had nothing!

I have been through some really hard times with my wife, when we did not have any money. We had to warn our visitors to sit in a particular way because our chairs were weak and broken. She even had to go abroad to work to buy us some furniture. I have truly struggled with my wife, so I love her. I did not have to wait until I was an old man to get married.

I love the people with whom I have been through struggles and difficulties. They are different from those who have come in a time of total blessing. When you are already established in life, you will have people interested in you because you are already blessed.

But the wife of your youth will marry you not because of what you have, but because of who you are. It is a blessing to marry young.

5. **Non-polygamous marriage**

And they were both naked, the man and his wife, and were not ashamed.

Genesis 2:25

The only person you must be naked with is your wife; not your girlfriend, fiancée, nurse or secretary. You are not supposed to have any other wife. God does not endorse polygamy. A polygamous lifestyle encourages fornication.

In Ghana, we have "official" polygamy, where a man maintains two or three wives. But there is an "unofficial" version of polygamy which is practised by most successful people in Ghana. They have an official wife whom they take to official functions and appear in public with.

There are also the unofficial women in the lives of these men. And this is common practice by most of the "big shots" in our society. Such men have no intention of divorcing their wives. They will spend the weekends at special places with these "side" girls. They travel with them to Paris, and generally have a good time with them. But they still maintain the official marriage.

We must keep this culture of unofficial polygamy far from us, if we want to avoid fornication.

6. Sexually active marriages

We need to have sexually active marriages. There are many marriages which are not sexually active. It is amazing that before people get married they want to hold and touch each other, but when they get married they can lie by each other like logs.

Why commit fornication when you can commit love.

Drink waters out of thine own cistern, and running waters out of thine own well.

Proverbs 5:15

Sex can be likened to drinking water. And we drink water several times in a day. So the Bible admonishes you to have sex several times, so you will not thirst for any other woman. There is more symbolic language in Proverbs 5.

Let thy fountains be dispersed abroad ...

Proverbs 5:16

26

What in sex looks like a fountain? God's rule for healthy marriages is that the fountains should be allowed to disperse abroad. You must allow the fountains to flow. Some fountains have been closed two weeks or six months. Such fountains are not blessed!

... and rivers of waters in the streets.

Proverbs 5:16

What could these streets be? If the fountains are going to flow into the streets, then God says:

Let them be only thine OWN, and not strangers'...

Proverbs 5:17

Let her be as the loving hind and pleasant roe; let her breasts satisfy thee at all times ...

Proverbs 5:19

If you are married, your wife's breasts must satisfy you at all times! Why should you be playing with somebody's breast, when you have your own wife's?

One of the ways to prevent fornication if you are married is to have sex regularly. When you eat and are satisfied, you do not feel like eating any more.

Women, especially, should know that when they have sex regularly with their husbands, they prevent them from having extramarital affairs. A man of God fell into sin. I was sitting with him after he admitted he had impregnated one of his church members; he was crying. I was so sad, and I wanted to know how it happened.

He described the difficulties of sex he had with his wife. She did not want to have sex with him. She kept complaining that she was tired, or cold. As soon as the husband committed adultery, she became active. She realized her husband's adultery was a product of what was going on at home.

Some wives are just waiting for their husbands to commit adultery and then they will wake up!

27

Chapter 5

Spiritual Keys to Avoiding Fornication

1. Honesty

You need honesty to save yourself from fornication. If you have a problem and need help, you have to be open about it. The doctor cannot help you unless you open up and tell him your problem. No one can help you if you do not ask for help.

Everybody *needs* help, but not everybody *wants* help. You need to open up and share your problems with honesty. Without the belt of truth and sincerity, you can never receive help from God.

There is a story about a Christian brother who always thought the messages preached in church were directed at others. The pastor would minister under the power of the Holy Ghost, and this Christian brother would sit in the church assuming it was for somebody else.

After the service, he would thank the pastor and say, "Pastor, bless you for this message. I believe you really ministered to *THEM*. You really touched *THEIR* hearts. It's a message *THEY* really needed." The pastor tried to modify his sermon so that the man would realize that he was actually talking to him but it was to no avail.

Then one day, it rained and there was a flood. No one but this brother came to church. As he sat there alone, the Pastor said to himself, "At last this young man will know that the message is for him."

The pastor preached his heart out. After that the brother came up and said, "Pastor, that was a very powerful message. If only *THEY* had come to church today, in fact, *THEIR* lives would have been touched!"

28

And that's how it is. We preach the Word, and people *always* assume it is for somebody else. We are simply not *honest* enough to accept that we have a problem.

2. Prayer

We need prayer to be able to deal with sin.

And said unto them, Why sleep ye? rise and pray, lest ye enter into temptation.

Luke 22:46

Prayer is very important to prevent you from falling into temptation. Prayer strengthens you for whatever is coming your way. Next time you fast, get up early and pray before the day begins. You will find supernatural strength to go on. This strength comes from prayer. When you pray, you build up your spirit and become spiritually strong.

The Bible says the body without the spirit is dead. That means the day your spirit goes out of your body, you will die. **It also means that whatever is happening in your body is affected by your spirit.**

It helps you to fight off certain temptations. That is why Jesus said you should pray, in case you fall into temptation. That is why Jesus prayed all the time. Once, Jesus prayed for forty days and nights. Soon after praying and fasting, the devil came to tempt Him, but He was too strong for the devil. The devil had chosen the wrong time to attack Christ.

Many years ago, the devil tried to bring a temptation my way. But that day, the Lord led me to pray for hours. I did not even know why the "tongues" seemed to be rolling out of me. That prayer delivered me!

The Bible says we do not know what to pray for as we ought. *Nobody knows what is going to happen tomorrow. But God knows! That is why He said we should watch and pray in case anything happens.* The disciples slept on that fateful night. All of them were tempted, and all of them fell. It is not only Judas

29

who forsook Christ on that night. All the disciples deserted their master in the day of His greatest need.

3. Deliverance

Some cases of fornication need deliverance. Other cases do not. If you are always being unfaithful to your husband or wife, you need to be delivered.

Some people, especially the chronic fornicators, need to see a pastor in order to undergo deliverance from evil spirits. If you have a chronic problem, then you need deliverance. If something drives you to fornicate, certainly it cannot be God who drives you.

... For oftentimes it had caught him: and he was kept bound with chains and in fetters; and he brake the bands, and was DRIVEN OF THE DEVIL into the wilderness.)

Luke 8:29

When something drives you to sin over and over again, you probably need deliverance.

It is only the devil who drives people. God does not drive people! God does not drive us. Even when you need to be saved, God will not force you to be saved. I believe that what we need to do is to be humble enough to admit that we need deliverance and ask our pastors to help us.

God does not force us to do anything. I have come to see that if YOU want to go to Hell, YOU will go to Hell and God WILL NOT stop you. I learnt years ago not to force people into Heaven.

God will not force you to get your deliverance; you must seek God yourself.

4. Seek grace and mercy

I think the grace of God is the most important factor. You may use all the other steps but you will still fall. You can use

30

every "mathematical" or logical step under the sun: deliverance, followed by honesty, plus sexually-active marriage and non-polygamous marriage, right through to early marriage, divided by a holy relationship, multiplied by a relationship unto marriage, to the square of no relationship!

It is by grace and grace alone!

The song writer said, "Through many dangers, toils and snares, I have already come. Twas grace that brought me safe thus far, and grace will lead me home."

Friends, it is grace that will see us through!

Chapter 6

What Is a Strange Woman?

And why wilt thou... be ravished with a strange woman...
To keep thee from the evil woman... the... strange woman.
That they may keep thee from the strange woman...

Proverbs 5:20, 6:24, 7:5

I first noticed the phrase, "strange woman" in the Bible some years ago. I was then a young Christian growing up in the Lord. I often wondered to myself, "What is a strange woman?"

We understand a strange woman to be an unusual person. But what is unusual about this person? What unusual things does this person do?

A Strange Woman Is a Destroyer of Precious Lives

For by means of a whorish woman *a man is brought* to a piece of bread: and the adulteress will hunt for the precious life.

Proverbs 6:26

This book is all about these hunters of precious lives! I believe that God will use this book to deliver the unsuspecting Christian from her deadly traps. I realize that the devil can recognize the precious life from afar. He knows when God's hand is on you, so he targets you. One of the devil's oldest and most successful agents is the strange woman.

Although our topic is "The Strange Woman", we also recognize that a man can be "strange". I am only using the female gender because the story in the seventh chapter of Proverbs depicts a woman who is "strange". This is a very important topic, because it is necessary for every Christian and minister to survive the journey of this life without falling prey to the common sexual sins of our day.

Strange people are those whose behaviour sows the seed of fornication, adultery, homosexuality, etc in others.

An innocent brother or sister, or even a man of God who has otherwise lived a pure life, can easily fall prey to these strange people. Strange people are not only in the world, but they also abound in the church.

The Bible calls her the strange woman. Some people call her the prostitute, but I prefer to call her the strange woman. Many people have had sexual experiences, even though they never planned to have them.

There are some men who hate certain women, because when they looked back they realized that there had been a long-term plan to destroy them! There are some ladies who lost their virginity when perhaps, they were too innocent to even know what was happening to them! Unfortunately, they had an encounter with a strange person.

As Christians, we do not war against flesh and blood but our enemy works through flesh and blood. The Bible has described these strange people in graphic detail. God wants us to know who they are, and to recognize this syndrome in ourselves.

Fornication is not an easy sin to deal with. Often those who get involved in fornication have a hard time overcoming it or ever stopping. Sometimes they are unable to ever overcome it. This therefore makes it a favourite area of attack by the devil.

Fornication is not only present in the world, but also in the church. Hundreds of ladies are ready to go to bed with their pastor if they get the chance to.

I remember when an altar call was made for ladies who had come to the church with the intention of enticing and tempting the head pastor. The response was amazing! Many ladies came and were prayed for. All these were strange women who admitted openly that they were hunting for the precious life of the pastor. There are four types of strange women.

1. The calculating strange woman.

This type of strange woman is the one who knows exactly what she is doing. She is conscious of who she is and what she is doing.

Her aim is to entice men, and to lead people into sexual affairs. Watch out for the calculating strange woman. She may look innocent and harmless but she is calculating and moving closer, step by step.

2. The unintentional strange woman.

This strange woman is not aware that she behaves like a strange woman. She has many of the symptoms and signs of "strangeness". Sometimes people grow up in a culture of lewdness and immorality. They inadvertently take on the characteristics of strange women. They dress in a half-naked way and do not think twice of it.

I remember attending a conference one day when a lady from another country gave a speech at a dinner. She stood by the side of her daughter and made a presentation to some of the most noble men of God of our day. Unfortunately, most of her breasts and her daughter's breasts were sticking out. Actually, it was just their nipples that were not showing. They were completely unaware of their presentation. It was so normal in the country where they came from. Indeed, your culture can turn you into a strange woman without your knowing what you are doing.

3. The professional strange woman.

The people in this group are known all over the world as prostitutes. Prostitution is one of the oldest professions in the world. Prostitutes are usually seen on dark streets and corners trying to entice people. Apart from the women who call themselves prostitutes, there are many ladies who would sleep with a man in exchange for a dinner, a pair of shoes or a nice outing. These are informal prostitutes but they are also prostitutes because they trade their bodies for something. There are people who get promoted in their jobs by sleeping with their bosses. In other words, they sleep their way to the top. Watch out for informal prostitutes. They abound in our modern world.

4. The spiritual strange woman.

Many churches are full of strange women. Women are naturally spiritual and they love to seek God for the security He provides. They speak in tongues, they read their Bibles but they also readily have sex with everyone.

The church is full of precious lives. The Bible says she hunts for precious lives (Proverbs 6:26). These precious lives are men and women who love God and who would serve Him with all their hearts. Satan is not just going to sit around and allow people to serve God. The more people serve the Lord, the more dangerous it is for Satan and his cohorts. Young people are the special targets of sexual demons.

Sex, is an act of the flesh. Sexual tastes, sexual appetites, and sexual styles are learned features of the flesh. Just as a man acquires the taste for certain foods in his youth, a man also acquires the taste for certain sexual experiences as a young person. It is usually difficult to get away from what you have learned in your youth. This is why people who grow up on a diet of sex, homosexuality or pornography find it very difficult to ever stop doing these things. Sometimes they try and try but the body has acquired the taste and needs to do it to be at peace. Sometimes, many years come and pass and you find a pastor descending into what he used to do as a youth. For instance, an African may be married to a European lady for many years. Sometimes thirty years after they are married he finally blurts out, "I am tired of this bread, salad and sausage and bland pepper-free sauces. I want some chilies, some stews and some fiery soups, some corn meal and some pounded yam." You see, the flesh has grown up on a diet of these things and it is not easy to get away from what your flesh learned to like.

This is why the strange woman's work is so significant. Once she is able to train you in sexual delights and exotic experiences, you will have a taste for that kind of excitement. Once you have been trained in watching strange women act out frenzied and energetic sexual orgies on pornographic films, your flesh may always have an appetite for it. Unfortunately, these appetites may be stirred up later in life.

When Satan identifies you as a precious life, he seeks to attack you through the works of a strange woman. Through a strange woman, a precious life will become an irrelevant life as far as the ministry is concerned.

Chapter 7

Signs of a Strange Woman

It is important for every Christian to be delivered from the snares and traps of strange people. In the Bible, particularly in the book of Proverbs, God has given us some of the signs by which we can identify a strange person and avoid her. I want to show you twenty signs of the strange woman. A strange woman may have some or all of these signs. Do not be deceived if a woman does not manifest some of the signs. This list of signs is just to help you pick out a strange woman from the crowd.

1. **A strange woman has a group that she identifies with.**

   ... a young man ... Passing through the street near her corner ...

                                                    Proverbs 7:7, 8

This story in Proverbs tells us that the naive young man went to her corner. The strange woman had a corner. **Strange people have their special corners.** They also have special groups of friends who congregate with them at these special places. Everybody has a friend. There is basically nobody without a friend. I have my friends, who are mostly pastors.

We know the proverb, "Birds of the same feather flock together", and "Show me your friend and I will show you your character." These sayings are not in the Bible, but they are true.

People flow together in groups, the like-minded with the like-minded, **friends with friends.** The secular strange women have their special corners. The Red Light District is a popular corner for strange people in any country. These are places where you are sure to find them.

My wife told me about a group of strange girls she knew when she was in school. This particular group of girls were all involved with married men, and they frequently met to compare notes. Sometimes one of them would be heard asking, "Have you asked him for the shoes?" Another would also say, "I have told him to buy me the plane ticket." They had something in common; therefore, they stuck together and influenced each other.

Strange people always move in special groups.

2. A strange woman operates at special times.

Proverbs 7:9 says she operates "in the twilight, in the evening, in the black and dark night".

The secular strange women operate in the dark and black night. The evenings are times when evil can flourish. It is rare to find them at their corners in the afternoon, but in the night they abound.

The black and dark night also speaks of the time of difficulty and stress. Many people encounter a strange woman when they are going through difficulties. The black and dark night speaks of times of pain, times of confusion, times of not knowing where to turn and what to do.

Also, you are a young man; you must not be in the company of certain people at certain times. **If you are in a relationship, there are certain times that you should not be with your beloved—(fiancée).** If you are a married man, you are not supposed to be at certain places with certain people at certain times. A married lady should never have a twilight dinner with her boss. Never!

In the church situation, **strange people usually do not attend evening Bible teaching meetings.** They are more regular at Sunday services, because that is when a lot more people come to church, and they can show off their best clothes. **You will never see such people at prayer and fasting meetings**, especially if it is going to last all night, or several hours.

They will however be the first to get ready if the church is going to the beach or some place to have a good time. Some of these people are bold enough to say they only go to church to trap a Christian man or lady!

3. A strange woman has a particular way of dressing.

... there met him a woman with the attire of an harlot ...

Proverbs 7:10

A strange woman dresses in a suggestive and revealing way. You can pick them out by their dressing. The Bible did not say she was a harlot, but that, she came with the dress of a harlot. If you are a Christian there are certain dresses that you are not supposed to wear. A believer ought to dress decently. If you are not a prostitute but you often dress like one, then you have one of the characteristics of a strange woman.

Strange women often dress in suggestive and revealing ways. It is not only the dress that speaks, but their pose also says volumes. You can immediately see they are after something. If you dare come to church with such a dress, then there is no doubt that you are strange. Some of the dresses expose half of the breasts. But a woman's breasts are not meant for public display. I know of only two reasons why breasts were made:

1. For breastfeeding, and

2. For husbands to enjoy!

Ladies, always dress decently—do not dress in suggestive or revealing ways! Make-up helps to enhance the beauty of women, but there is a limit. At a point the make-up becomes too much and other messages are loudly sent across.

Every Christian should look beautiful, but we should be careful not to cross the line into "strangeness". The Bible says temptation shall surely come, but woe to him through whom the temptation comes.

4. A strange woman has had sexual and romantic relationships with a good number of men.

... MANY strong men have been slain by her.

Proverbs 7:26

As Christians, we should not just set eyes on people, fall in love and marry them. No! There is more to Christian marriage than love at first sight!

During a pastoral visit to New Jersey, I became acquainted with an elderly African-American woman. In her house, she pointed out photographs of her children to me. She said she was blessed with sons who were all preachers. However, she said she had lost one of her sons recently.

She said her son, a pastor in New York had gotten married to this beautiful lady. Before the marriage they had done the AIDS tests, but both were negative. So he went ahead and married the lady. However, some months into the marriage she developed full-blown AIDS, with terrible diarrhoea, weight loss and all the usual symptoms.

This old lady told me how she tried to make her son break up the marriage. He refused, and died a few months after his wife. Dear friend, this pastor married someone who probably had a bad history – a strange woman! And he did not even know it! He paid for it with his life.

Another Christian brother had a beautiful wedding, but later when he was alone at home with his wife, the Spirit of God revealed horrible things about his wife to him. He suddenly realized that she was not what he thought she was. He was shocked to find out that she had slept with many pastors and mighty men.

I am not saying that you should not marry somebody who has a history per se. But you must know about her past life in order to guard yourself.

You should remember that a strange person can continue in the same ways even after marriage.

5. A strange woman is striking. You will notice her!

She is loud ...

Proverbs 7:11

Watch out for ladies you notice. They strike you and you remember them. She who strikes you has also struck many other men. The striking characteristics of this strange woman have made many men come after her like flying insects after a bright light. Strange women are loud and that is why they are noticeable. There are various ways of being loud. It could be verbally or in appearance. You will also notice such people through their loud dressing, giggling and loud laughter.

There is a type of dressing that literally shouts, making all eyes turn to look at you. In the church, there are those you just cannot help but notice. They probably want you to notice them anyway. Do remember, **"She who strikes you has already been struck!"**

When I was in Achimota School (a secondary school in my country), there were times when we had to walk from the eastern compound to the western compound. On some occasions I had to walk behind a group of girls. I often walked faster and overtook them. But as I walked a few metres ahead of them I would hear them giggling.

I had no idea what they were laughing about. I would often change the way I walked, but the giggling and laughter would only grow louder. After a few of such experiences, any time I saw these girls on the way, I would make no effort to overtake this loud and strange group. Remember that a woman with a meek and quiet spirit is considered precious in the sight of God.

6. A strange woman is stubborn.

She is ... stubborn;

Proverbs 7:11

Stubbornness is a symptom of witchcraft. A witch is usually stubborn and resistant to advice, instruction and input. She is unbending. She is unyielding and she does not give up. The strange woman syndrome goes along with this landmark symptom of stubbornness!

41

The Bible says the wife should submit to her husband. The word submit means "to yield, bend, agree, or to obey". A good wife is supposed to yield, but if she is a strange woman, she will be stubborn. **God's order is for the husband to lead, and the woman to follow.** But in these days of women's liberation and the Beijing Conference, you have all sorts of women rising up to fight every established authority!

Dear women, you are not wiser than God. No matter what you think and know, and no matter the theories you come up with, there can be only one head in a home. Any animal with two heads is abnormal and a freak.

A strange woman is a dangerous person to marry. She is stubborn in the church, stubborn at home and stubborn at work. She always has a reason or an excuse for not doing what she ought to do.

Watch out for ladies who cannot be convinced and do not change their minds. Watch out for the unyielding, unbending sisters. You may be dealing with a strange woman. Pharaoh was so stubborn that God had to speak to him through flies, frogs, deaths, tragedies and disasters! You do not need to go through similar experiences. Do not be too hard and do not be too stubborn. These are traits of a strange woman.

7. **A strange woman is always going out.**

... her feet abide not in her house:

Proverbs 7:11

Strange people do not like staying at home. A woman is supposed to be "homely", to be able to take care of and manage the home.

... that the younger women marry ... guide the house ...

1 Timothy 5:14

This also means the wife must know how to cook and supervise people in the house. There are some Christian sisters who do not know how to cook, because they are always in church, and are never at home.

In fact, it is a tragedy to marry a woman who cannot cook! When your stew is set before you, you will not be able to tell the difference between that and soup! This is often the fate of the men who marry strange women. They are condemned to a life of eating in misery every day.

One of the attractions of going home after a hard days' work is the food at home.

8.   A strange woman is a hunter.   She wants a man!

Now is she without, now in the streets, and lieth in wait at every corner.)

Proverbs 7:12

When a woman wants a man she is always outside in the streets, lying in wait at every corner for an opportune time to strike. Such women can only be satisfied when they are with one man or another.

... the adulteress will HUNT for the precious life.

Proverbs 6:26

In the Proverbs 7 story, the strange woman acts as if she was lying in wait for this particular man. However, if the naive young man refuses her, she will lie in wait for the next man and tell him the same story—as if she was waiting particularly for him.

9.   A strange woman loves physical contact.

So she caught him and kissed him ...

Proverbs 7:13

Strange people like to touch others. They often hug, kiss and press some part of their body against the people they are after. When you are walking with them, they never want to leave you. They always want to hold or hug you.

The strange woman knows that generally, a man can be sexually aroused by sight. She is also aware that a man will find it difficult to resist a woman's touch. **In order to conquer her victim totally she will cause him to yield by touching him.** Some Christian brothers and sisters also have the habit of holding on and hanging on to each other. Watch out!

10. A strange woman is bold and unlawfully familiar.

... kissed him ... with an impudent face ...

Proverbs 7:13

The strange woman is very bold and unlawfully familiar with the man she wants to have. Why do you talk to somebody about intimate things, when you are a just an acquaintance?

Strange people try to get close—in fact too close for comfort. Unless you are at a certain level of closeness with the person, you do not even have the right to comment about their hair or body. As soon as you become unlawfully familiar with somebody, you have crossed certain borders. Strange women effortlessly move out of their boundaries.

11. A strange woman is not ashamed.

Now is she without, now in the streets, ...

Proverbs 7:12

She comes out in the open, into the street to solicit, and is not shy or ashamed of her behaviour. I was in Geneva once with one of my associate ministers, and we were talking seriously with a brother in a restaurant. This happened to be near a place where prostitutes lurk, and there was this prostitute who was such a nuisance that we had to usher her out.

Initially, she did not want to go out, so we called the police, and eventually she was driven away. Later on we were busy talking, when one of the other prostitutes came along in a coat. She stood right in front of the whole restaurant, and opened up her coat to reveal her stark naked body. This lady had no shame.

Unknown to us, when the first one went out, she told all the other prostitutes that we had sacked her and so this other strange woman had come to taunt us. Strange women have no shame. They have been naked and undressed with *many* men under *many* circumstances *many* times! The strange woman has no shame.

If you are a woman, and you do not mind exposing your body, your breasts, your thighs, or any part of your body, then you are *strange*! You may think you are being fashionable, but in reality, you are just what the Bible calls strange. Unfortunately, there are born-again Christians who are not ashamed to expose themselves this way.

12. A strange woman is full of deception.

With her much fair speech she caused him to yield, with the flattering of her lips she forced him.

Proverbs 7: 21

The lies of a strange woman are part of her arsenal. A lie is a window into the darkness of a malignant soul. A lie is a symptom of many hidden evils.

A strange man may say to you, "I love you. You are everything to me. Look, I'm going to marry you anyway, so if you love me, show it! I love you, that's why I want to sleep with you. I just want to express my love for you." So with these and other such lies, a man can talk his way into your life.

My pastor used to say that if any man tells you he loves you and wants to express his love to you by sleeping with you, *tell him he can express his love for you by buying you chocolates!*

On the other hand, there are women who also flatter men, especially powerful men. Some are very experienced in praising pastors. She will tell you that you are such an anointed man of God. **With such seemingly harmless words, a strange woman can work her way into an unsuspecting man of God's heart.**

Faith comes by hearing, so when you continue to hear such words, you will eventually believe and yield.

13. A strange woman appeals to you through food.

I have decked my bed with coverings of tapestry ...

Proverbs 7:16

The word "bed" in the Hebrew is "arsi", which refers to a dining couch, and not a sleeping bed.

She was saying that she had laid the table. So this strange woman was appealing to the young man through food. **Such strange people will often invite those they target to eat with them.** If you are a young single brother, you may be exposing yourself to such strange people if you just go about eating all over the place.

A pastor visiting his members must remember that his business with them concerns the salvation of their souls. You are not supposed to go around eating from home to home. To some extent the saying is true that, *"The way to a man's heart is through his stomach."* Food is good, but it can be used to trap you.

Eat thou not the bread of him that hath an evil eye ...

Proverbs 23:6

Sometimes your stomach can contribute to your fall.

As a Christian, a pastor, and a husband, I do not go out to lunch with just anybody. Once, I saw a Christian brother who already had a fiancée, sitting with another lady over a candlelit dinner. I was very surprised, because he was inviting trouble for himself. I really did wonder if he would still marry his fiancée.

14. A strange woman speaks of her interest in sex.

Come, let us TAKE OUR FILL OF LOVE UNTIL THE MORNING ...

Proverbs 7:18

Many husbands pray that their wives would come up to them and say, "Honey, I want you now!" Some Christian wives could learn a lesson or two from strange women!

Many wives are not prepared for sex—or do not want it. So it is an exciting thing for a man to meet a woman who wants to have sex with him. **If a woman comes to a man and indicates that she wants to have him, it appeals to him greatly.**

15. A strange woman is a stranger.

Say unto wisdom, Thou art my sister; and call understanding thy kinswoman: That they may keep thee from the strange woman, from THE STRANGER *which flattereth with her words.*

Proverbs 7:4-5

You genuinely do not know much about a strange woman. She is mystical about her past and gives vague answers to all your questions. When you ask her how many men she has slept with she will say "one or two" when in actual fact she has slept with one or two hundred. A strange woman is full of surprises. One secret leads to another. Your life with a strange woman will be a life of discoveries. You will make newer and more discoveries about your partner as the years go by. In the end you will discover you never really knew her.

On the night of his engagement a man was told that his wife-to-be was actually a suicide bomber. He did not believe what he was being told. But as he reflected on this shocking information he realized that he knew hardly anything about her. Such is the world of a strange woman. She is indeed a stranger and you cannot know the life she has lived in the past or the world from which she has come.

16. A strange woman loves to appear to be spiritual or religious.

I have peace offerings with me ... have I payed my vows.

Proverbs 7:14

There are strange women in the most spiritual sections of a church. I once knew a top prayer warrior who was a senior strange woman. By her own count and in her own words, she had slept with over two hundred different boys. And yet this strange girl was the most prayerful sister in the church. People's apparent spirituality does not mean that their holiness is real.

The strange woman said, "I am also a believer." She was using every means to convince him that she was also a believer— just like him. There are many strange believers in the churches, even the charismatic ones. She said she had paid her tithes.

This was a very cunning strange woman who knew that her victim was a religious person. She knew that she could never come near him unless she behaved like a spiritual person. So she presented herself as someone who was obedient to God's commands: She had already paid her vows and made her peace with God.

17. A strange woman captivates with her beauty and her eyes.

Lust not after her beauty ... neither let her take thee with her eyelids.

Proverbs 6:25

She is beautiful, and she knows it. A strange woman enhances her beauty in a striking way. You must not allow yourself to be taken in by her eyelids. When you make eye contact with somebody, you can speak to the person. It is a form of communication. That is why I look at peoples' faces when I am preaching. I am communicating with them. The strange woman, with practice over the years, knows how to effectively communicate her carnal intentions to a man.

The Bible warns us not to lust after her. So if you notice that she is beautiful, that should be the end of the story. Do not lust after her beauty! Lust is an animal desire for sexual indulgence.

18. A strange woman is slippery and sly.

... the lips of a strange woman ... smoother than oil:... her ways are moveable ...

Proverbs 5:3, 6

A strange woman is not straightforward; all her ways are movable and shaky. Ecclesiastes 7:26 says, "I find more bitter than death the woman, whose heart is snares and nets. ..."

As a pastor, if you cannot identify the strange women you can easily fall prey to them.

There are strange women who come to the pastor with their numerous problems. They are also easily given to tears. If you are not experienced, you will take out your handkerchief and try to comfort her. The strange woman is taking advantage of the pastor's love and kindness.

The Bible says her heart is full of ideas and traps. When you are a young man you sometimes do not know when you are walking in the midst of them. Some ladies come to church and in no time at all, a young man proposes to them. Sadly, many young men are looking for the most beautiful face. A young man can easily fall into these traps, and end up marrying a strange woman.

In the same way, Christian ladies are impressed by the outward appearance of strange men, and accept their proposal, only to be taken on a strange tour!

19. A strange woman is attracted to great men.

...many strong men have been slain by her.

Proverbs 7:26

Years ago, my pastor friend told me that girls were attracted to important or great men. He said to me, "When you play instruments, stand on stage, or are a leader, you are likely to be an attraction to strange women." Each classification of great people—pastors, singers, businessmen, heads of states, and so on have their own kind of strange women who are attracted to them. Therefore, if God is raising you up, you must beware of these strange people. **It is my prayer that God will deliver you from the snares of strange people!**

Chapter 8

Strange Women in The Bible

A strange woman is a person who corrupts and spoils the church, and the ministries of individuals. The Bible has many examples of women that were used as weapons to corrupt and destroy God's servants.

Seven Strange Women of the Bible

1. THE CLASSIC STRANGE WOMAN: THE STRANGER, THE HUNTER, THE EVIL WOMAN

For the lips of A STRANGE WOMAN drop as an honeycomb, and her mouth is smoother than oil: But her end is bitter as wormwood, sharp as a twoedged sword. Her feet go down to death; her steps take hold on hell.

Lest thou shouldest ponder the path of life, her ways are moveable, that thou canst not know them.

Hear me now therefore, O ye children, and depart not from the words of my mouth. Remove thy way far from her, and come not nigh the door of her house: Lest thou give thine honour unto others, and thy years unto the cruel:

Lest strangers be filled with thy wealth; and thy labours be in the house of a stranger;

And thou mourn at the last, when thy flesh and thy body are consumed,

And say, How have I hated instruction, and my heart despised reproof;

And have not obeyed the voice of my teachers, nor inclined mine ear to them that instructed me!

Proverbs 5:3-13

To keep thee from THE EVIL WOMAN, from the flattery of the tongue of A STRANGE WOMAN.

Lust not after her beauty in thine heart; neither let her take thee with her eyelids.

For by means of a whorish woman a man is brought to a piece of bread: and THE ADULTERESS WILL HUNT FOR THE PRECIOUS LIFE.

Proverbs 6:24-26

Keep my commandments, and live; and my law as the apple of thine eye. Bind them upon thy fingers, write them upon the table of thine heart.

Say unto wisdom, Thou *art* my sister; and call understanding *thy* kinswoman: That they may keep thee from the strange woman, from the stranger *which* flattereth with her words.

Proverbs 7:2-5

These passages are the basis of this book. They outline the characteristics of a strange woman and the effect she will have on a person. Remember three things about the classic strange woman.

Remember that she is a stranger; you do not really know her. She tells you part of her story to keep you happy and to deceive you into thinking that you know who you are with.

Remember that she is an evil person no matter how beautiful she looks. Beauty is not usually associated with evil. We associate beauty with nice and happy things. But the Bible calls her an evil woman. When you meet a strange woman, remember that you are encountering well-packaged and well-presented evil.

Also remember that she is actually hunting you, even though you may think you are after her. It's amazing, but the strange woman is actually hunting a man the way a lion would hunt for an antelope.

2. LADY TAMAR

Tamar was a strange woman because she made God's servant have a child with her even though he had no intention of having a child with her. She knew exactly what she was doing and before Judah was aware of what was going on, he had impregnated her.

51

A woman who lies in wait and tricks you into having sex and into having a child is also a strange woman.

Why would a man think that you are a prostitute? Why would a man think that you are available for sex? This lady, Tamar, gave these two messages very successfully. Watch out for women who give these messages.

And she put her widow's garments off from her, and covered her with a vail, and wrapped herself, and sat in an open place, which is by the way to Timnath; for she saw that Shelah was grown, and she was not given unto him to wife.
WHEN JUDAH SAW HER, HE THOUGHT HER TO BE AN HARLOT; because she had covered her face.
And he turned unto her by the way, and said, Go to, I pray thee, let me come in unto thee; (for he knew not that she was his daughter in law.) And she said, What wilt thou give me, that thou mayest come in unto me?
And he said, I will send thee a kid from the flock. And she said, Wilt thou give me a pledge, till thou send it?

Genesis 38:14-17

3. LADY MICHAL

Lady Michal was given to charm King David and to cause him to fall into a trap. When a woman is on a mission to snare a man, she is a strange woman. The Bible tells us that the woman, Michal, was intended to be a snare to David. No wonder he shook her off in the day she mocked him for dancing before the Lord. Perhaps he was led to disconnect from her because her whole existence was to be a snare to King David.

Now Michal, Saul's daughter, loved David. When they told Saul, the thing was agreeable to him.
And Saul thought, "I WILL GIVE HER TO HIM THAT SHE MAY BECOME A SNARE TO HIM, and that the hand of the Philistines may be against him." Therefore

52

Saul said to David, "For a second time you may be my son-in-law today.

1 Samuel 18:20-21 (NASB)

4. LADY DELILAH

Delilah is perhaps the most well-known strange woman of the Bible. Her conquest of Samson and her destruction of his ministry is a famous but sad story. Through her soft laps and enticing words she overcame the reasoning faculties of Samson and brought him to his knees. Oh, how powerful is the lure of sex to the starving and desirous man! It is this weakness of all men that the strange woman preys upon.

> And it came to pass afterward, that he loved a woman in the valley of Sorek, whose name was Delilah.
>
> And the lords of the Philistines came up unto her, and said unto her, ENTICE HIM, AND SEE WHEREIN HIS GREAT STRENGTH LIETH, and by what means we may prevail against him, that we may bind him to afflict him: and we will give thee every one of us eleven hundred pieces of silver.
>
> And Delilah said to Samson, Tell me, I pray thee, wherein thy great strength lieth, and wherewith thou mightest be bound to afflict thee.

Judges 16:4-6

> And when Delilah saw that he had told her all his heart, she sent and called for the lords of the Philistines, saying, Come up this once, for he hath shewed me all his heart. Then the lords of the Philistines came up unto her, and brought money in their hand.
>
> And SHE MADE HIM SLEEP UPON HER KNEES; and she called for a man, and she caused him to shave off the seven locks of his head; and she began to afflict him, and his strength went from him.

Judges 16:18-19

5. THE STRANGE WOMEN OF BALAAM

But I have a few things against thee, because thou hast there them that hold THE DOCTRINE OF BALAAM, WHO TAUGHT Balac to cast a stumblingblock before the children of Israel, to eat things sacrificed unto idols, and TO COMMIT FORNICATION.

Revelation 2:14

These women of Midian were used by the prophet Balaam to entice the men of Israel to have sex with them. When they had sex with the women they fell out of favour with God and opened the door for the devil to destroy them. Once again you will see the pattern is the same; use the strange woman who does not mind sleeping with any man to cause the precious life to fall. God's judgement against the strange woman is usually very severe.

And Moses said unto them, HAVE YE SAVED ALL THE WOMEN ALIVE? Behold, THESE CAUSED THE CHILDREN OF ISRAEL, THROUGH THE COUNSEL OF BALAAM, TO COMMIT TRESPASS against the LORD in the matter of Peor, and there was a plague among the congregation of the LORD.

Now therefore kill every male among the little ones, and KILL EVERY WOMAN that hath known man by lying with him.

Numbers 31:15-17

6. THE STRANGE WOMEN OF THE INVADER

But he who comes against him will do as he pleases, and no one will be able to withstand him; he will also stay for a time in the Beautiful Land, with destruction in his hand.

And he will set his face to come with the power of his whole kingdom, bringing with him a proposal of peace which he will put into effect; he WILL ALSO GIVE HIM THE DAUGHTER OF WOMEN TO RUIN IT. But she will not take a stand for him or be on his side.

Daniel 11:16-17 (NASB)

In this Scripture, a young woman was given as an act of war. Knowing the power of sexual desire as well as the power of women to corrupt, the women were openly used as weapons of war to destroy the enemy. Every minister of the gospel must recognize some women as weapons of war deployed against him.

7. THE STRANGE WOMAN OF BABYLON

For true and righteous are his judgments: for he hath judged the great whore, WHICH DID CORRUPT THE EARTH WITH HER FORNICATION, and hath avenged the blood of his servants at her hand.

Revelation 19:2

And IN HER WAS FOUND THE BLOOD of prophets, and of saints, and of all that were slain upon the earth.

Revelation 18:24

Rejoice over her, thou heaven, and ye holy apostles and prophets; for GOD HATH AVENGED YOU ON HER.

Revelation 18:20

The woman of Babylon is shown in Revelation chapters 18 and 19 to be a person who is filled with demons because of her fornications. She is judged for living deliciously and having sex with so many kings of the earth. Not only did this woman have sex with many kings, but she also destroyed the lives of holy apostles and prophets. Through this woman's life huge ministries were destroyed and many souls could not be saved. It is no wonder that her judgement is so severe in the book of Revelation. Perhaps a great lesson from these texts should go to the women who lend themselves to destroy men through sex.

The sexual leanings and tendencies of men are well known by experienced strange women who exploit them and destroy them through that. It seems that God recognizes the weak frame of the men and rather poured out his judgement on the strange woman of Babylon. In the final revelation we see how God was so angry with the strange woman of Babylon. He destroyed her with much fire and brimstone. The kings of the earth stood aside and marvelled at such destruction meted out to the woman. God called the the apostles and prophets His holy apostles and. All strange women should take note of this word because it is a prophecy of the doom of all strange women who tempt God's servants.

Chapter 9

Ten Keys to Understanding Your Attraction to Women

1. Understand What Beauty Is

The unspoken cry of many young men is: "I see a beautiful girl! I want to have a beautiful girl! I want to marry a beautiful girl." However, many young men do not understand their attraction to women.

God is very concerned about who you get attracted to. The person you get attracted to may become your girlfriend or your wife. She may then destroy you or she may help you.

Many things are going to happen and much "water is going to pass under the bridge". **Will your marriage make you or break you?** This is what God is concerned about.

When God was instructing the Israelites, He was very concerned about whom they became attracted to. He knew that those who became close to the Israelites could turn their hearts away from Him. *God knew that the wife would influence the husband and the husband would influence the wife.* I am a married man. I influence my wife and my wife influences me. It's as simple as that.

Sometimes men think that as the head of the home they will always lead the way. But you must realize that your wife does influence you.

Solomon was a great man. He had seven hundred wives and three hundred "official" girlfriends. (Imagine how many baby dedications he had to attend)!

Solomon was a wise man. One day, Solomon prayed to God in a way that really touched God's heart. He didn't ask for money or a new car; he rather asked God to give him wisdom to be a good leader. God was so touched that He decided to give Solomon more wisdom as well as all the riches he did not ask for.

My brother, can you see that Solomon really loved God? Can you see that he was really called of God? And yet, in his latter years Solomon began to backslide. He became a fetish worshipper. He became an idol seeker. He left the ministry and resigned from his church.

For it came to pass, when Solomon was old, that his wives turned away his heart after other gods: and his heart was not perfect with the LORD his God, as was the heart of David his father.

1 Kings 11:4

He started well, but ended badly. How could this happen to Solomon? The answer is simple. *Solomon married the wrong women!*

First of all, some of his wives were not believers. Secondly, although some of them were, they were lukewarm. Some of his girlfriends did not love the ministry as much as he did. Remember, Solomon had the purest of motives. No one ever prayed like Solomon did.

Some of the ladies just loved the glamour of being married to King Solomon. They didn't mind being the 21st or 75th wife. All they wanted was the position (many women are position-minded).

After many years, the effect of the wrong marriages and wrong relationships began to tell. Solomon was not as strong as he was before. He could not continue quarrelling with his wives over church. Solomon was tired of arguing about where to go for fellowship. Solomon wanted peace in his old age. So he just "flowed" with his backslidden wives.

My dear friend, if this is what happened to Solomon whose name is in the Bible, what do you think will happen to you? If you make the mistake of getting attached to the wrong person, you may live to regret it.

The spiritual brothers will say, "Oh, I love her, because she's so spiritual."

The aristocratic brothers will say, "Oh, I love her, because she's so educated."

The Goobley-Gob tribe will say, "I love her because she is from my tribe."

Whether a man is spiritual or not, he is attracted to the beauty of a woman.

Marriage is something you must not take lightly or wantonly, but soberly and in the fear of the Lord, duly considering the causes for which marriage was ordained.

Since physical beauty is so powerfully attractive, it is important to understand how it works. If you do not understand it, it will overpower you and lead you along a dark, dangerous and slippery path.

2. Understand That Beauty Is Important

... beauty is vain ...

Proverbs 31: 30

Beauty contains the power to attract you. From this verse, you might conclude that beauty is not important. **But that isn't true. Beauty is vain, but very important.**

Why then is beauty vain? Beauty is vain because it will fade.

An elderly lady once came to my church to minister. She took out a photograph of a very beautiful young girl and asked the congregation to identify her. Everyone said the photograph was a picture of her daughter. Her reply was a big surprise. She revealed that she was the one in the photograph. This elderly lady had changed so much with the passage of time. Her beauty had faded away.

The old lady said to us, "Look how ugly I am."

She went on to make the point that life was like a vapour, appearing for a short while and then disappearing. I realized how temporary beauty really was. Beauty is vain because it will fade. If all you look for in a marriage partner is beauty, then when the beauty begins to decrease with the years, you will look for another beautiful face. Although beauty fades away, it is still important, because whoever you marry must look nice to you! After all, you will look upon her until you die.

This is the secret every woman must know. Your beauty is important in getting and keeping your husband's attention. If you had to look good to get him, then you will have to look good to keep him!!

Some Christians who feel they are being led by the Holy Spirit do not look at the beauty of the person they choose. Do not make the mistake of closing your eyes when choosing a partner.

But the Bible tells us:

... she[or he] is at liberty to be married to whom she will ...

1 Corinthians 7:39

You must marry somebody whom you want to marry!

Do not marry somebody just because she was recommended to you. You must be satisfied and happy with what you see. You are going to live with that person. Marriage is something you must enjoy and endure. You must marry somebody who looks nice to you!

When I first met my wife I thought she was the most beautiful person in the world. And I still think she is. Her physical beauty has always been important in my attraction to her. Beauty will count in your happiness and satisfaction in marriage.

3. Understand That Everyone Is Beautiful

Every woman is beautiful. Every woman has the power of attraction. There is nobody who is not beautiful in one way or the other.

I will praise thee: for I am fearfully and wonderfully made ...

Psalm 139:14

Everyone has some beauty about him or her. You should never think that you are not beautiful. God took time to design you, to create your nose just the way it is. Perhaps He made your ears small, and your lips as full as they are.

God has not made you a disappointment or a disaster. He does not make such things.

If you are short, being short is beautiful. If you are black, being black is beautiful, and if you are white, being white is equally beautiful.

I am black, but comely ...

Songs of Solomon 1:5

I do not know what you are, but God made you that way. Look at yourself in the mirror, and admire yourself. There is no need to change any part of your body.

Accept what you are, and believe that you are beautiful because God made you. Some ladies think of themselves as ugly because someone teased them when they were young. Maybe in school they called you names. So although you have grown into a beautiful young lady, you still believe those lies.

Do not listen to those lies; they are just jealous of you. When people tease you, they are probably jealous of you because you have something they do not have. You must begin to appreciate beauty in everything that God has made. Some people are not happy with what they have. But there is some beauty in every man and in every woman.

Look at yourself in the mirror again and say, "Lord, I thank you because I'm beautifully and wonderfully made!"

4. Understand That Beauty Lies in the Eyes of the Beholder

As an African, I have often wondered how similar Chinese people looked. Sometimes, I have not been able to tell the difference between two Chinese women. Sometimes they look alike, having the same eyes, same face, and same skin colour. This is my perception.

However, a Chinese man will be able to see the difference. To him, some of the Chinese ladies are strikingly beautiful and some are even ugly. But to an African they may all look the same.

In the same way, a Chinese man may not be able to tell the difference between two Africans. So we judge beauty by what we have been taught by our society. Our environment affects our perception.

The typical African will be looking for certain physical features before concluding that a woman is beautiful. He may be looking at how plump she is, how big her "bomboms" are! The European might be looking for a woman who is thin and tall!

I chose my wife because, to me, she is beautiful. Beauty therefore depends on who is looking. Be confident about your choice, since it depends on you.

Beauty depends on who is looking. So be confident about your choice.

5. Understand That Each Age Has Its Beauty

There is the beauty of a sixteen-year-old girl that a thirty-year-old woman does not have. There is the beauty of a thirty-year-old woman which is different from that of a sixteen-year-old. There is a beauty of the forty-two-year-old lady, and another beauty of a fifty-six-year-old. *At each age, a person possesses a particular beauty.* Therefore, there is no need to wish that your wife or husband would be sixteen years old again.

Each age has its own type of beauty, which cannot be repeated. You cannot become young again!

The beauty of each age is given by God. You can never rewind to the beauty of a past age. You cannot go backward and you cannot go forward. You are what you are.

Some people think that you can only be beautiful when you are very young. But that is not true. I know some beautiful fifty-year-old ladies. And I know some beautiful sixty-year-old ladies. At each stage of your life God makes you attractive.

6. Understand That Beauty Is Like a Flower

... if she pass the FLOWER of her age, and need so require ... let them marry.

1 Corinthians 7:36

Attraction has a point at which it blossoms like a beautiful flower. Most plants have a flowering stage. And the plant which flowers is the one that is attractive to both insects and humans.

The same can be said about a woman. There is that age in a woman's life we call the flower of her age, or the flower of her beauty. That is when you are most noticeable. That is when you are most beautiful, and when men propose to you. For some women, this stage comes for a short while, but for others the period is longer. Unfortunately, the development of the mind and maturity of most Christian sisters does not correspond to the development of their beauty. This leads many of them to reject the right partner.

When they are at this stage, a brother may propose to marry them and they would laugh it off.

Just because you are in the flower of your age should not make you laugh at people who want to marry you. You keep tossing the suitors away. You make jokes about them. You show others the letters they wrote to you. But what you do not know is that this period does not last forever. You must not only use your emotions. You need to use your mind. Rely on the Spirit of God and wise counsel to know when to marry and whom to marry.

Remember that the peak of your beauty and attractiveness is indeed like a flower—it is temporary.

Many ladies miss the opportunity to get married. They miscalculate during the "flowering" stage of their lives.

All of us have a stage at which we are most attractive. It is given by God for a season and a reason.

7. Understand That Attraction Depends on Many Factors

Everyone God has made is beautiful. But this beauty can be enhanced by several factors. Beauty depends on your hair, your dressing, your make-up, and even the time of day or month.

But if a woman have long hair, it is a GLORY to her ...
1 Corinthians 11:15

The beauty, and therefore the attraction you see in a lady can increase or decrease depending on certain things. A lady's dress today may make her look outstanding. Her hair style tomorrow may make her lose marks. Even the mood of the lady affects her looks! Pimples are often caused by emotional disturbance.

Beauty depends on many factors, so invest in those factors.

The Christian wife should not use pregnancy and babies as an excuse for being careless about her looks.

Some husbands do not even care what their wives look like! But you admire other people's wives on television. As a good husband, you must be concerned about your wife's clothes because her attractiveness depends on that.

Many young men become confused about the looks of their fiancée. They wonder, "Did I choose a beautiful girl?" They oscillate in their feelings towards her. What is happening here is that they are confused by the normal variations in beauty and attractiveness. If all that you are looking for in a woman is physical beauty, you are likely to be confused.

8. Understand That External Beauty Depends on Internal Beauty

Outward beauty depends on the inward beauty. If you are beautiful inside it shows on the outside. Sometimes I see people and I know that they are not doing well spiritually.

I saw two pictures of a lady who had converted from witchcraft to Christ. One photograph showed her when she was practising witchcraft, and the other when she had accepted Christ. They were two different people. When you are doing well spiritually, the beauty of it shows outwardly.

Proverbs 7:11-27 describes a strange woman who is very attractive on the outside, but very stubborn and loud. Such a person is beautiful outside but ugly in character and emotions. Some people, especially unbelievers, try to polish their outside whilst they are so nasty on the inside.

Young men, look for inner beauty. The Bible calls it "a meek and quiet spirit".

A beautiful wife once threatened to slap her husband in public. She was definitely a beauty on the outside but a tigress on the inside.

Young men, do not be impressed by what you see on the outside. Look out for the inner beauty. In spite of the fact that my wife is *physically* beautiful to me, I saw something *inside* her that attracted me—the inner beauty. When a person has a good spirit, and a good heart, it adds to the person's beauty.

9. Understand That Beauty Is Given in Portions

Live joyfully with the wife whom thou lovest all the days of the life of thy vanity ... for that is thy portion...

Ecclesiastes 9:9

You need to realize that beauty comes in portions. Everyone has a portion, but nobody has it all. Your portion is what you are entitled to. Your portion will include some things, but not everything. You cannot have a black and a white wife in one person. Your wife may be an excellent cook, but she could have problems with being a hostess when your friends come home.

That is your portion, and God expects you to be content with her.

You may know a friend's wife who is very good when visitors come home. You may admire the way she receives, chats and talks with the guests. You may appreciate her confidence and range of knowledge on political issues. But you may find that she is not able to cook very well. Her stews may be like soups, and her soups like stews! But God expects you to be content with your wife, including her weaker points. Be content!

No matter how hard you look, you will find out that your portion has its strong points and its weak points.

The Bible tells you to enjoy life with your portion. You can't have it all. So accept your portion and enjoy it, because that is the way God intended it to be.

Do not reach out for somebody's portion because everyone is entitled to only one portion. One man, one woman. Remember the Genesis story:

And the Lord God said, It is not good that the man should be alone; I will make him an help meet for him.

Genesis 2:18

Adam had only one portion—Eve, and not Eves. Adam was not given Rose, Rosemond, Rosalyn, Rosemary, or Roseanne. He was given only Eve.

You are not allowed to have two portions. When you go to a party and you have been served with some food, you may realize that your portion of rice is larger than your neighbour's. But if you look closely, you will find that your neighbour's piece of chicken is larger than yours.

You dare not stretch out your hand to take your neighbour's portion of chicken, because you have your own portion.

You must learn to be satisfied with the portion that God has given you.

10. Understand That Spirituality Is Preferred to Beauty

... beauty is vain: but a woman that feareth the LORD, she shall be praised.

Proverbs 31:30

The Bible compares a beautiful woman with a woman who fears the Lord. If you ever have to choose between beauty and spirituality, choose spirituality.

Your portion may not be so beautiful, but very spiritual. Your woman may have certain godly characteristics. Choose that! If ever you are faced with such a decision do not hesitate to choose the godly woman, because it is the woman who fears the Lord who will be praised.

Once you are married you will confirm the fact that beauty is always secondary to godliness.

The spiritual person who knows and fears God will become more and more attractive to you as the years go by.

Beauty has very little to offer, apart from what you see. But the spiritual person has her faithfulness, her character, and godliness to offer you.

You may not believe it, but just ask those who have gone a bit further down the road, "Which one is more important?"

Beauty or character?

Beauty or spirituality?

Beauty or integrity?

If your wife does not pray, you are in trouble.

Find a woman who prays. Find a woman who is deep into the things of God. If you marry a greedy, selfish and lazy woman, you will find yourself living in hell. You will suffer, not because she is not outwardly beautiful, but because she is inwardly ugly.

A person who is ugly inside but beautiful outside can be compared to a cemetery. A cemetery is well decorated with flowers, but as you come a little closer and go deeper, you will see dead men's bones and teeth sticking out.

A woman without a godly character looks nice on the outside but go a little further and you will find an angry, lazy, and devilish person. Be careful, my brother. Go for the spiritual person.

Chapter 10

The Danger of a Dual Life

Woe unto you, scribes and Pharisees, hypocrites! for ye are like unto whited sepulchres, which indeed appear beautiful outward, but are within full of dead men's bones, and of all uncleanness.

Matthew 23:27

Duality is practised by people who have received Christ but do not change completely. They do not allow their conversion to affect every aspect of their lives.

Duality is the state of living a life with double standards. It is the state of having two personalities or two natures embodied in one person.

You are practising duality when you have one lifestyle in public, and another one in private. This happens when you are not ready to sacrifice and live for Jesus Christ.

Duality is the spirit of hypocrisy, the spirit of lies and the spirit of self-deception.

One of the greatest forms of deception is self-deception. When you are a fool and you don't know that you are a fool, your situation is worse than a fool who knows that he is a fool!

Often, when I counsel people and can get them to understand the problem they are faced with, much of the work is already done. When doctors are able to diagnose the sicknesses of patients, eighty per cent of their work is done.

Self-deception is very dangerous and comes about by repeated lying. When you knowingly and continuously lie, you begin to believe the lies.

Self-deception occurs when you do something wrong, but repeatedly tell yourself that what you are doing is right.

In the end, you will believe when you commit sin, that you are actually doing the right thing. You have done it so many times and for so long that, you have convinced yourself it is the right thing.

During the dark years of Nazi Germany, the Nazis convinced themselves that killing Jews was right. At a point they believed that the Germans were really a special race which was superior to every other race. They also believed that all their problems were caused by the Jews.

Then they came up with what they called the FINAL SOLUTION: How to solve the Jewish problem. They believed in it, preached it, taught it in schools and they gradually eliminated as many Jews as possible. They must have believed it with all their hearts, because they killed the Jews consistently. They murdered millions of people.

Unfortunately, there are so many Christians who are two people in one. Some years ago, I used to be a musician and moved around with many other musicians. Many of them had two personalities.

When they stood on stage they would sing songs like, *Amazing Grace, I Love You Lord,* and many other beautiful songs. But if you met them off stage, their lives were something else. At a point, I was no longer impressed with any gospel singer.

There are many singers and choristers who sing beautifully, but have unholy private lives. They have two lives! One life is evident when they sing and lift up their voices to the Lord. The other life is portrayed when they are off stage. Indeed, some of these singers can even bring you to tears. But then, when you get closer, you wonder if they are even Christians.

Your life on stage should conform to your private life. If someone comes to live with you, he should discover that the character on stage is the same as the one at home.

Pastors can easily have a double life. Some ministers would even admonish the congregation not to copy their lifestyles!

Some ministers say to their congregations, "Do what I say, but don't do what I do." What a shock!

Chapter 11

Ten Types of Duality

**Even so ye also outwardly appear righteous unto men,
but within ye are full of hypocrisy and iniquity.**

Matthew 23: 28

There are many ways in which people practise duality. Jesus'
strongest rebukes were for those who practised this particular
form of deception. It is a particular evil that we must all fight
against. In this chapter, I want you to study the different ways in
which this evil can creep into your life.

1. Separated and unequally yoked

Wherefore come out from among them, and be ye separate,
saith the Lord, and touch not the unclean *thing;* and I will
receive you, And will be a Father unto you, and ye shall be
my sons and daughters, saith the Lord Almighty.

2 Corinthians 6:17,18

Samson was a perfect example of someone with a dual life.
His dual behaviour was classic and every Christian can learn
something from his story.

He had a religious, separated side of him, which was shown
by the fact that he never cut his hair. Yet, he was unequally yoked
to the things of the world.

There are Christians who appear separated from the world,
but yet live in sin.

**Samson's life was one that was separated and yet he was
entangled in the world.**

He was separated because he was a Nazarite—that is, someone
who was not supposed to live like the rest of the people. He was
unique, in the sense that he was not supposed to drink, or cut his
hair. He didn't cut his hair, and it was a sign of his consecration

to God. All those around him thought he had nothing to do with the world. It was an open sign to everyone that Samson was a Nazarite, separated unto God. He never drank, and everybody knew him in that way.

However, at the same time, he wanted to have an unbeliever wife (Judges 14: 2-3). He was a man anointed of God, yet he wanted to play with worldly pleasure.

And there are many people doing that today. Many of us pastors have two personalities and two lives. There are also many church members who have two personalities.

There is the personality that is displayed when they walk through the church gate: holier than everybody else. Once they get out of the church gates into their homes or offices they live their different lives.

Some of you reading this book are just like that. You are in the church and you claim to be born again. Your friends think that you are a believer, but on the other hand, you are playing around with the world. Your best friends are unbelievers, which makes you just like Samson.

You are in a born-again church where you hear life-changing sermons over and over again, and yet your best friends are unbelievers.

If your friends at school and at work are openly declared non-Christians, you have a big problem!

I remember when an unbeliever boasted, "Every Sunday, I pick up a girl from these born-again churches. I just have to pass by the junction after church on Sunday and give one of them a lift, and I'll have somebody to sleep with."

Samson also played with God. He wore the long hair, which was a sign that he was a member of a Christian church, but he still dabbled in fornication with the world. Apparently separated, but also with the world.

I can just see Samson with his long hair as he walked through town. Everybody knew that meant that he was an anointed man of God, separated unto God, walking in the things of God and a member of the church. However, he wanted to marry an unbeliever.

When he told his father who he wanted to marry, he asked, "Is there no woman in Israel you can marry?"

Samson replied, "Oh no, this non-believing girl is the one I want."

How can you even think of marrying a complete outsider when you know you are a believer separated unto God?

2. Spiritual and carnal

Because the carnal mind is enmity against God: for it is not subject to the law of God, neither indeed can be.

Romans 8:7

Samson was a spiritual person and yet he was carnal. At certain times he gave the impression that he was very spiritual. At other times, it was surprising how carnal he could be.

You wonder if this carnality and spirituality could be in one person?

... the Spirit of the LORD began to move him at times ...

Judges 13:25

The Spirit of God was upon the man and yet he was carnal. He was so spiritual that he was the spiritual leader of Israel for twenty years! However, we realize that he had a woman problem: He was a playboy although he had the Spirit of God.

I remember a man of God who used to play this kind of game. He was a powerful preacher, and I was really moved every time he ministered. Yet, this man was also playing around with many of the women in his church.

One day, whilst fornicating with one of the women, she asked him, "So, after doing this with me, how will you be able to preach tomorrow?"

He replied, "When I sin like this, then the anointing comes even more."

There are people who commit various sins just before going to church. And really, it does not make any difference to them. Such people could even be the most expressive when they are in church. They are spiritual and at the same time carnal.

Look at Samson; he loved to go out for prostitutes. He slept with one woman after the other. He did all this, in spite of the fact that the Spirit of God was upon him. For twenty solid years he was in the ministry, and yet he was plagued with these problems!

3. Mighty and weak

If your pastor knows that you are weak, he can pray for you but if you pretend to be mighty, how can he know that you need help?

If you are weak, but present yourself as strong, you are preventing your own deliverance. You are covering what needs help. When you appear strong even though you are weak, nobody can help you.

As a pastor, I have come to see that there are people I don't particularly need to visit, because they are strong! But then sometimes there is a weak one, and I have to rush there because he needs attention. When you look strong like Samson, you won't get any attention.

Samson was mighty in ministry, killing thousands. At the same time he was a weak man when it came to his private life. He was mighty publicly but the opposite in private.

In the book of Judges we see how Samson carried the gates of the city on his shoulders. What a mighty man! In this sense he was not weak. He was so mighty that he killed one thousand people with a jaw bone. However, he allowed Delilah to take

75

advantage of him. She overcame the mighty man because he was also a weak man!

The Philistines recognized this weakness also, and capitalized on it to eventually conquer Samson.

Are you both mighty and weak? My brother, please don't be both mighty and weak.

Many public officials are like that. In their public life they look so dignified and so respectable. When they are interviewed on television, they sound so powerful but in their private lives, they are morally weak.

4. Nasty and nice

So you, too, outwardly appear righteous to men, but inwardly you are full of hypocrisy and lawlessness.

Matthew 23:28, NASB

There are some people who are very nice when they are in public, but are nasty when they are at home. Their spouses and children know them to be very impatient and abusive, but those outside the home see them as the nicest people on earth. There are people who complain that their spouses respect the pastors more than their own husbands. They cannot help but notice the humility and gentleness which their wives reserve for their pastors and outsiders.

These people have two different natures: the nasty nature, which they display in private (usually those close to them have to endure it), and the nice nature which they display in public.

Amazingly, some of the nicest people are also the nastiest. Perhaps, it is a reflex to camouflage their nastiness at home. Such people take extra precautions to appear nice to outsiders, especially those they meet for the first time.

5. Mature and yet childish

That we *henceforth* be no more children, tossed to and fro, and carried about with every wind of doctrine, by the sleight of men, *and* cunning craftiness, whereby they lie in wait to deceive;

Ephesians 4:14

Samson judged Israel for twenty years. It takes maturity to be a judge, and to be able to lead a nation for this number of years.

Looking at Samson's life, you may get the impression that he was just lustful, chasing one prostitute after another. However, he was a judge for twenty years. That is maturity in ministry.

Samson had another side of his personality, which made him behave like a child. In the book of Judges, we read how he caught three hundred foxes and tied their tails in pairs. Then he set them on fire and sent them into the Philistines' farms. This was Samson's revenge on his father-in-law for giving his bride to his best man.

His behaviour was childish. Indeed, there are simpler ways of burning a farm. The man was clearly childish in his thinking, and yet at the same time, he was a very mature man who presided over Israel.

There are many Christians like that. Their level of understanding of God's Word is excellent; yet they are so childish. A child is very unsteady and unstable. A child cannot sit at one place for a long time. There are many childish Christians who despite their knowledge of God's Word, cannot settle down in any church. Today, you will meet them in this church, the next time, you will find them in another church. They just cannot belong anywhere. They are unsteady and unstable, yet they have great knowledge. It takes maturity to belong to a church.

One Sunday evening, I tuned in to a Christian talk show (on the radio) on my way home from church (I usually leave church very late). That night, the discussion was on churches and pastors. As I listened to the discussion I marvelled at how wise and mature the arguments sounded.

Then I suddenly recognised the voice of one of the contributors. He was one of the most unstable Christians I have ever known.

He had once been a member of my church, but had since moved to at least two other churches. This fellow had such wise comments to make on the behaviour of pastors and churches, yet he was like a child — unable to belong to any church for a long period. Perhaps, he knew too much to belong anywhere. He was mature and yet childish.

Another feature of a child is that it cries a lot. Children are often easily hurt, and need a lot of time and attention. In the church setting, anybody who behaves like this is a child.

Such people know a lot of Scriptures and have been Christians for a long time, yet they still get easily hurt. A mature person doesn't seek attention, but rather gives it.

Maturity is needed in every facet of our lives. It takes maturity for a man to settle down with one of the many beautiful ladies he sees around him. That is why people respect married men. It takes maturity to settle down. A child cannot settle. That is why a man who does not want to settle may not be regarded as a man yet. He is still a boy.

6. Loyal and slanderous

Likewise must the deacons be grave, not double-tongued ...

1 Timothy 3:8

There are people who claim to be loyal and yet are slanderous. They have two tongues: one speaks good and the other evil.

The Bible describes duality of the tongue as being double-tongued. There is only one animal that seems to have two tongues—the snake!

Some years ago, I was in a fellowship meeting when the pastor took a second offering. I complained about the taking of two offerings to a sister sitting by me. She gave me a look that shut me up. When I saw her face my heart smote me and I realized I had said something wrong.

After the service, I went up to the pastor and confessed to him what I had said. He was very surprised. Stretching out his hands, he told me God was going to use me.

But I could have complained bitterly about the man of God only to tell him how much I enjoyed his sermon afterwards.

He may have been impressed with me but I would have been "stabbing him in the back", pretending to have a loyal tongue.

A person with an accusing tongue is a follower of the devil.

... the accuser of our brethren ... which accused them before our God day and night.

Revelation12:10

7. Worshipping with your mouth, yet rebelling in your heart

God is sick of duality and of all forms of pretense. When the Israelites practised duality, God became so angry that He refused to accept their sacrifice.

He asked:

To what purpose is the multitude of your sacrifices unto me ... Bring no more vain oblations; incense is an abomination unto me ... I cannot away with ...

Isaiah 1:11, 13

God was tired of their hypocrisy, and told them that He would not heed their prayers because they lived evil lives even though they offered so many prayers.

God said, "Away with it! I cannot, and I do not want it."

Truly, there are so many Christians who sing, lift up their hands, and tell the Lord that they love Him—but these are often empty words.

Many women feel dejected when they realize that the man who claimed to love them had been lying all along. Some women become so heartbroken that they cannot believe the words of any man for the rest of their lives.

God also does not take it lightly when your heart is far from Him but you outwardly appear to love Him.

8.   Goodness and badness

The dual person exhibits both goodness and badness.

... your goodness is as a morning cloud, and as the early dew it goeth away.

Hosea 6:4

The morning cloud and the early dew are things that appear for a short while and then vanish almost immediately. Some people would know a dual person to be evil. Another group of people would know him to be a very good person.

If you went to the home of a person living a dual life, the members of his family would readily supply you with tales of his evil deeds. But if you went to his colleagues at work they would tell you of his goodness and kindness.

The goodness of such a person is temporary, and is only revealed to a selected few. Those living dual lives might appear to be good, but their goodness is short-lived.

9.   Men pleaser and God pleaser

Is it possible to please God and men at the same time? Paul states:

... for if I yet pleased men, I should not be the servant of Christ.

Galatians 1:10

According to Paul, if he pleases men, he cannot please Christ. It is as simple as that! There is no way you can please men and also please God.

When I responded to the call of God on my life, I displeased my parents. Think about it!

You sent your child to school and he qualified as a doctor. Would you be pleased if he decided to become a pastor instead?

At the time I took this decision, my church was very small and unimpressive.

If you want to please men, you will never be a servant of Christ. To avoid living a dual life, you may sometimes have to go contrary to man's opinion, and just please God. If your parents want you to marry an unbeliever just because he is wealthy, you will have to go contrary to their desire, because the Bible commands us not to marry unbelievers! Your family may not be happy, but God will be pleased with you.

Are you pleasing men or pleasing God?

10.   Impressive and unimpressive

Therefore judge nothing before the appointed time; wait till the Lord comes. He will bring to light what is hidden in darkness and will expose the motives of men's hearts. At that time each will receive his praise from God.

1 Corinthians 4:5 (NIV)

God cannot be fooled by our duality. Even if we impress men, He will judge us with righteous judgement. His judgement will be based on the things we have hidden which no one can see. Most of us want people to be impressed with us. We wish the people around us would be impressed with what we have; our cars, our appearance etc. The person you must aim to impress is God.

The person living a dual life will do and say everything possible to impress his friends and those around him.

Sometimes, people go to the extent of going for bank loans in order to live a certain kind of lifestyle to impress friends.

Many people live above their means because they want to present a certain image of themselves.

The person living a dual life may be regarded as wealthy and living in luxury—when in reality, he is living on borrowed glory.

Soon his creditors will catch up with him, and the image he has built around himself will come crumbling down! That is when the people he has deceived will be disappointed and unimpressed with him.

It is good to be liberated from that constant desire to impress others!

If I had tried to impress people, my church, Lighthouse Chapel International would not have gotten to this stage.

I would have spent our income on impressive cars, clothes and lifestyle, trying to impress those on the outside.

There is no need to impress anyone. With time, people will get to know who you are, what you are, and what you are made up of! It is just a matter of time!

Do not be impressive on the outside and unimpressive on the inside.